Balanced on Purpose
The Story of Seven Cows

Kenneth Mwale

ISBN: 9781920562434

Published by Practical Truth Library
P. O. Box 14427,
Lyttelton, 0140
Pretoria,
South Africa
Tel: 0724236990

Contents

Introduction
My Own Seven Cows Story

On the 7th of August 2009, I put in my resignation as senior pastor of a Church that my wife and I had planted five years prior. After five years of pastoring this Church, it was clear that my time pastoring this particular church had come to an end. Difficult as it was, the decision had to be made for me to enter another phase of my life.

On this windy August afternoon, I wrote a one-page resignation, and emailed it to my bishop letting him know that I was stepping down as senior pastor of the church. I offered to stay for up to six months to help with a smooth transition period for the installation of a new pastor. The events that followed are not important to include in this book, but I must say they taught me a lot about human nature. I learnt from this experience that I am stronger than I thought and that people are not what they usually project themselves to be. However, the lessons that I learnt during my time of reflection after this episode are the most important. They actually led me to write this book.

My resignation was followed by six very interesting years before I entered a phase of my life that I think is a fulfillment of a prophecy I got in the year 1999 in a church service in Kimberley, South Africa. During these six years, before I stepped into my current role, I did a lot of things, which was quite a new thing to me, because I always knew myself as a pastor.

I was a consultant, facilitating management workshops. I was a broker, putting business deals together, and I was what you can call a freelance preacher, if there is such a thing, preaching here and there when some people asked me to. I also wrote two books in the process, and ran seminars about the principles I wrote in the books.

My previous years prior to this six-year period were defined by people knowing me as a pastor, but now I didn't have that one thing that I was doing. I was a consultant, and a businessman, and still some people called me pastor, even if I wasn't pastoring any church.

My biggest dilemma during this period was how to define myself. It was difficult for me to put a handle on what I was becoming. People who knew me in my pastoral days called me Pastor Ken. Those that knew me in the world of consulting called me Ken. A few people that I was brokering business deals for just knew me as a Zambian guy with a lot of business connections. I often got calls from people asking me to connect them with some of my business connections. My children didn't know what I did and I am sure that, as little as they were, if someone asked them what I did, they would have told them they didn't know but that "he is away from home a lot". My wife should have been the most confused to say the least.

During these years I felt like I was living outside my element, as it is said when someone is not fulfilling their purpose with what they are doing. I was not being me. Although I was doing a lot of things, most of which were quite successful, I was not focused on anything that would define who I am. During this period I made a few big deals that landed me some good money, and did a lot of travelling conducting workshops in different places here in South Africa and Zambia, but still I could feel I was out of my element. I love to teach, and I love travelling which I was doing a lot in my new consulting gigs, but something was continuously nagging me at the core. I started to feel like the Children of Israel who couldn't sing the Lord's song because they were in a foreign land.

"By the rivers of Babylon we sat down; there we wept when we remembered Zion. On the willows near by we hung up our harps. Those who captured us told us to sing; they told us to entertain them: "Sing us a song about Zion." How can we sing a song to the LORD in a foreign land?"[1]

Nonetheless, in all this, one thing remained constant. I still held on to my faith in God, and still spent time with Him in prayer on a regular basis and one of my travelling companions was a Bible I won in a competition in Zambia in 2003. I settled my family in a church in the east of our city where we got our spiritual nourishment. Little did I know that this church was going to usher me into the next phase.

In my distress, I started to do some introspection. The Lord was kind enough to help me discover the source of my distress. He showed me that the source of my distress was contained in the

---

[1] Psalm 137, Good News Bible

story of the seven cows found in the book of Genesis chapter 41.

The story is about how a king's dream saved a young man from a prison sentence, and how the young man ended up becoming the prime minister of the land he was prisoner in. During his tenure he saved his new country from a deadly famine.

I now know that the power in the pages that follow will save many from a life that is undefined, a prison that many people live in. A life out of balance. Those people who will humble themselves and see the power of this story will be saved from a lot of pain in their present circumstances, or may be spared future pain.

Here is the story:

After two years had passed, the king of Egypt dreamed that he was standing by the Nile River, when seven cows, fat and sleek, came up out of the river and began to feed on the grass. Then seven other cows came up; they were thin and bony. They came and stood by the other cows on the riverbank, and the thin cows ate up the fat cows. Then the king woke up... Joseph said to the king, "The two dreams mean the same thing; God has told you what he is going to do. The seven fat cows are seven years, and the seven full heads of grain are also seven years; they have the same meaning[2].

This story forms the theme of this book. The first important thing to take note of is that the cows in the story are seven, not fourteen. Even if there are seven thin and seven fat cows, there are only seven cows shown that appear as either thin or fat. That will become clear as we continue. The story is about seven years that can be thin or fat, depending on how you live your life.

God showed me that the seven cows in the story represented the seven spheres of my life. Each cow stood for an area of my life. These areas, though distinct, make up a whole. These areas could either be thin or fat. The fat cows represented the healthy areas of the whole, and the thin cows represented the areas in which I was struggling—which means that I could have three healthy areas, represented by three fat cows, and four struggling ones represented by four thin cows. This was a light bulb moment for me as it helped me to start looking at my life from a

---

2. Genesis 41:1-4; 25-26; Good News Bible

bird's-eye view to see which of the seven areas of my life were thin and which of them were fat.

It gets interesting because as the story goes. God showed me that the areas of my life that were thin, just as it happened in the Biblical story, were eating the areas of my life that were fat.

As I did some deep introspection, I saw that during my years as a pastor in my previous pastorate, I concentrated on my family, my career as a pastor, my relationships, and my spiritual life. I had four fat cows. I neglected my finances, my health was in bad shape, and I had no social life at all to express personal hobbies and interests. These were my thin cows.

It became clear that my pain was due to the fact that I had neglected to take care of three areas of my life, and now they were eating up the areas of my life which I had concentrated on feeding. The result was pain, in the very areas that I had concentrated on. My marriage was in turmoil because I was always on the brink of bankruptcy financially. With every month that came, I had to negotiate my way with my landlord. I was behind my son's school fees, sometimes by three to four months. My health started failing, and I develop a severe case of ulcers and started living on antacid over-the-counter tablets.

After what God showed me, it was easy for me to see that what I was going through was a result of the areas of my life that I had neglected. Now these areas, like the thin cows in the story, were hungry and eating up the very ones I concentrated on feeding.

Because of this revelation, I started to see this same pattern in many people's lives. Others had great careers, stable financial lives, but had neglected their relationships, their marriages, and their health. I started to see how, because of their concentration on career and finances, their bad relationships and marriages were starting to affect their fat areas, which were their finances and career success. I saw in their eyes the same pain I felt, except that for them it was coming from a different source. The Lord then said to me that they were in just as much pain as I was; it just had a different origin. The principle was the same. They were feeding different cows from the ones I was, but still, the ones they were neglecting were eating their fat ones.

This revelation is what brought about this book and the Balanced on Purpose Workshops which

I am running everywhere, trying to help as many people to avoid the pain that comes from unbalanced lives. As you read the pages that follow, please pay particular attention to the Lord's still, small voice as He puts some light on some areas of your life that are either already bringing pain, or will soon do if you don't do something about the direction you are going. This book may just be a solution to your pain now, or a preventative against your future pain.

Just to give you a heads up. I want this book to be as practical as possible to you. Therefore, I have ended every chapter with a journal that I call "Balancing on Purpose". Take some time to answer some questions as well as reflect on the chapter and write down anything that you took out of the chapter. That will help you as you intentionally use the information to Balance your life.

Chapter 1
We All Have Seven Cows

We have adopted what I call a Babylonian way of thinking. The danger of this way of thinking is that it separates our spirituality and our physicality. It makes life look like the two are a sum of each other, not a whole. As a matter of fact, life is a whole made up of the two not a sum total of the two.

This attitude of separation is also responsible for what I will call a life of disintegration. What I mean by this is that, if you hold this way of thinking, chances are that you will look at certain aspects of your life as important to God and others as not. Those that aren't you won't take seriously, while those aspects that you consider important to God, you will take seriously. Life is a whole, not a sum total of different aspects. This means that all aspects of our lives are equally important.

On the other hand, if you are not a God fearing person, you will take those areas that you deem important seriously and neglect the ones that you feel are not. Either way, neglecting the spiritual and concentrating on the physical has the same results. Pain.

I want us to look at a passage of scripture that will help us to understand that our lives are an integration of seven spheres. These areas or dimensions are all equally important. They are all important to God, and so they should to you. God wants to be involved in each of the seven areas, not just a few. He expects you to look after each of these areas equally.

"The seven fat cows are seven years, and the seven full heads of grain are also seven years; they have the same meaning"[3]

The story that I told as I began this book is about how God showed me that, as a human being, I live within seven spheres. These dimensions are interrelated. They are not compartments, but an integrated system that makes one whole. They have no boundary lines. They mesh as one but we live in them interchangeably. That is why they can be

3. Genesis 41:26; Good News Bible, E-Sword

separately mentioned but cannot be separated. The truth is that, as human beings, we live in these spheres simultaneously. We are not the sum of these dimensions, but one whole that has many dimensions. While it is difficult to explain, the truth is simple to understand.

Our selves are like water, which is made from two component elements to make one whole. We also are multi-dimensional, and these dimensions make a whole. Although water has two components, you can't poison one part of water and have the other still remain fine.

The spheres of our lives include:

- ✓ Our spirituality
- ✓ Our Health
- ✓ Our Relationships (*These are relationships apart from our relatives, we can also refer to them as friendships*)
- ✓ Our Family (*including relatives*)/Marriage
- ✓ Our Career/Business
- ✓ Our Finances
- ✓ Our Hobbies

Some people may look at these dimensions of our being and trivialize the importance of some. What they don't know is that they do so at their own peril. Understanding how to successfully live healthily in all these dimensions is the very essence of what life is all about. To be happy, fulfilled, and pain-free, one can't ignore the fact that all these areas need to be healthy. I have yet to find a fulfilled, happy person who has some areas healthy and some in bad shape. Our happiness and fulfillment is relative to how healthy all of these areas are.

I want us to have a brief look at each one of these areas to provide a foundation for what will follow after this chapter.

Spiritual Sphere

A lot of people confuse a healthy spiritual life with religious activity. They think that spirituality and religion are one thing. Wrong. Most religious people are not spiritually healthy at all, and being spiritually healthy does not mean being religious. Most people do not know what real spirituality looks like. That is why the story of the Babylonians in Genesis 11 (which is discussed in a following chapter) comes in very handy.

In Genesis 11, people did not want to involve God in their everyday lives. They built a city for themselves, and built a tower as a place where they met God. Everything else in the city was their own thing. The only time God came into the picture was when they entered the tower. Sound familiar?

When we bring this situation home, we will see that even today. Many people find it hard to involve God in their day-to-day lives. They cannot imagine a God who wants to be involved in everything they do. They don't realize that every human activity is both physical and spiritual at the same time. There is no such thing as spiritual and physical reality; the two make up reality. Reality is made up of physical and spiritual. In Genesis 1, the Bible says "God created the Heaven and the Earth." In the original language, this passage means that God made spiritual and physical things.

To confine God only to what we deem spiritual is an insult to Him because He created both the spiritual and the physical. We have even come up with a term to classify what is spiritual and what is not. We call some things secular, and others sacred. Secular activities are not important to God and the sacred are, so we say. This is a very wrong way of looking at reality. God created everything and the best way of classifying things is not secular and sacred, but good and evil. There is evil and there is good. There is no secular and sacred reality, just good and evil. And every reality belongs to God. It is part of our being human. God is God of all reality.

When I think of a spiritually healthy person, two things comes to mind. The first is that a spiritually healthy person infuses their spiritual attributes into their day to day life. They don't just look at spiritual virtue as a way of appeasing God, or a passport to Heaven. They don't use their spiritual attributes and virtue to just stay in God's good books, but as a way of living. Spiritually healthy people live their spirituality.

A spiritually healthy person uses such virtues as love, forgiveness, patience, etc., as a way of life. In Galatians 5, Paul lists seven virtues that can help a person to live a spiritually healthy life.

But the fruit of the Spirit is: love, joy, peace, long-suffering, kindness, goodness, faith, meekness, self-control; against such things there is no law[4].

---

4. Galatians 5:22-23; Modern King James version Bible

These spiritual virtues are not religious practices. These are virtues that, when applied in life, enrich someone's life. The problem is that these virtues are looked at as simply religious practices. Even science is starting to realize that a person who has these virtues stands a higher chance of succeeding in their other aspects of life like career, relationships, and marriage.

Another aspect of a healthy spirituality is the dimension of gifts found in 1 Corinthians 12. Again we look at these gifts specifically as a tool to make our religious lives more exciting. These gifts are associated with religion, not with day-to-day life. Both in Corinthians and Romans Paul lists some gifts that God has given to us to use in our lives.

"Then having gifts differing according to the grace that is given to us, if prophecy, according to the proportion of faith; or ministry, in the ministry; or he who teaches, in the teaching; or he who exhorts, in the encouragement; or he who shares, in simplicity; or he who takes the lead, in diligence; or he who shows mercy, in cheerfulness"[5].

---

5. Romans 12:6-8, Modern King James Version Bible

"But there are differences of gifts, but the same Spirit.... For through the Spirit is given to one a word of wisdom; and to another a word of knowledge, according to the same Spirit; and to another faith by the same Spirit; and to another the gifts of healing by the same Spirit; and to another workings of powers, to another prophecy; and to another discerning of spirits; and to another kinds of tongues; and to another the interpretation of tongues. "[6].

I look at the virtues in Galatians as spiritual virtue that enhances our relationships as we interact with our fellow human beings. The ones in Romans and Corinthians are more related to our relationship with work or business. They help us with how we contribute to society. We shouldn't confine these gifts to religious activity.

---

6. 1 Corinthians 12: 4 -11; Modern King James Version of the Bible; E-Sword.

Health Sphere

"...do you not know that your body is a temple of the Holy Spirit in you, whom you have of God? And you are not your own...."[7]

Health is one of the areas that most people take for granted until they get sick. Popular culture looks at the body primarily from a physical point of view.

However, the scripture we quoted above shows that our body houses the Spirit of God. If our bodies are spiritual dwellings, it means that they are so important, and we need to look after them as such. God dwells in our bodies, and when our bodies are sickly, they don't make the best place for God to live.

There are three things that are very important when it comes to our bodies. The first is that, for us to maintain healthy bodies, we need to eat right.

Secondly, to keep our Lord's temple in tip-top condition, we need to rest enough. Rest is not something we do just because night has come. We rest so that we can prepare ourselves for work. We don't rest because we are tired. We rest so that we

---

7. 1 Corinthians 6:19; Modern King James Version Bible; E-Sword

can prepare our bodies for maximum performance. We work from a rested position; we don't rest after work.

Thirdly, our bodies need to be exercised. God created us such that we should give our bodies some physical application. In our modern lives, because we don't walk a lot and do less physical work, we need to deliberately engage our bodies in doing something physical. When we don't, we risk them becoming susceptible to disease. When we are out of shape, we have less energy. When we have less energy, our minds are affected and that also affects our work. That can start a vicious cycle.

Another important reason why we need to exercise is the ability that exercise has to condition our minds. When we push our bodies in exercise, and achieve certain milestones in our exercise regimes, we condition ourselves to win. If you tell yourself that you will do 50 push-ups and push your body to doing it, your brain is conditioned to achieving results. That can be translated into other areas of your life.

Relationships Sphere

"I have no strength left to save myself; there is nowhere I can turn for help. In trouble like this I

need loyal friends– whether I've forsaken God or not"[8].

Great friendships are not just for fun. As humans we are social beings. We cannot live all by ourselves, just as Job says in the above scripture. We have a need for connection, love, physical touch, and emotional contact with others. We enhance our own well-being by building strong networks of friendships around us.

Someone once said, "'a problem shared is a problem halved'? Truth is; Happiness shared is happiness squared". It is amazing that when we share our joy with those we love, we feel even more joy. This can only be true if we have great relationships. We also need others to help us maintain balance in life and comfort us in difficult times.

However, we should not forget that it is equally important to differentiate between healthy and damaging friendships. Some relationships are not good for us. We need to take deliberate steps to nurture great ones and cut those that are toxic. To have great friendships, we need to make time for each of them. We have to be intentional. We need to deliberately work at making the connections strong.

---

8. Job 6:13-14; Good News Bible; E-Sword

Our Family/Marriage Sphere

"Marriage is to be honored by all, and husbands and wives must be faithful to each other. God will judge those who are immoral and those who commit adultery".[9]

"...ruling his own house well, having children in subjection with all honor".[10]

"God setteth the solitary in families...."[11]

Having and enjoying a great marriage and a well-adjusted family is our heritage as God's people. It is part of being complete. When God blesses you with children, it is His will that they be well-adjusted

Wanting to be whole and complete, humans long for great intimacy in marriage as well as great relationships with siblings or one's own children. We have to deliberately cultivate a great home and family life.

---

9. Hebrews 13:4; Good News Bible
8. Hebrews 13:4; Good News Bible; E-Sword
10 Timothy 3:4; Modern King James Version of the Bible; E-sword
11 Psalm 68:6; King James Version of the Bible; E-Sword

Another very important reason why God values family is that it is a very big influence on passing on values to the next generation. God has entrusted parents to raise their children in the fear of the Lord. There is extensive research that shows that a person's chances of struggling with personal identity are increased when they are raised outside a family unit. The first models in someone's life are that person's parents.

Our Career/Business Sphere

"Don't build your house and establish a home until your fields are ready, and you are sure that you can earn a living""[12]

Every human was created by God to express themselves through some form of a vocation. It is everyone's God ordained mandate to experience success in their career. When God created man, the first thing He did was to give him a career. Career success is not just for earning lots of money, although that is part of what it does, but it is for our self-expression. Go to work to make a difference in

---

12. Proverbs 24:27; Good News Bible; E-Sword

someone's life, and money will be a spin-off from a successful mission to make a difference.

To gain respect and personal fulfillment, a man should in one way or another serve other humans and his family. Therefore, to be whole and complete, a human needs to have a steady business or career through which he or she expresses their God-given gifts and talents.

"Make it your aim to live a quiet life, to mind your own business, and to earn your own living, just as we told you before. In this way you will win the respect of those who are not believers, and you will not have to depend on anyone for what you need"[13]

Ask someone who is unemployed, and you will know that what I am saying is true. There are few things that can be as dehumanizing to a man as not making a meaningful contribution to humanity. Making a meaningful contribution is one of man's top needs.

---

13. 1 Thessalonians; 4:11-12; Good News Bible

Our Financial Sphere

"Feasting makes you happy and wine cheers you up, but you can't have either without money."[14]

There are few things in life that have the power that money has, and yet most people live in denial of that fact. Most people don't have good things to say about money, but when you dig deep into their psyches, their hate for money is not because of money itself, but the fact that they don't have enough of it.

People usually talk about what money can't buy, but they ignore the fact that there are things that can only be bought by money which are essential to our lives. I agree that money can't buy certain things, and yet I am also for the idea that, like the other six things in the seven core areas of life, money is one of those things that is equally important. Just as other things have their place and are important, money has its place and is also important. We can't go around putting our heads in the sand and talk bad about money when money plays such an important role in our lives.

---

14. Ecclesiastes 10:19; God News Bible; E-Sword

Our biggest problem is that we like to compare apples with pears. I will be the first one to admit that there are things that money can't buy. But that does not make money less important. To expect money to buy things that it wasn't meant to be used for is like expecting our health to buy us a house. Health is important because of areas where it is important, and money is important because of areas of our lives where it is important. We are not saying money buys everything; we are saying there are things only money can buy and those things are essential for life.

To have a whole life, one needs to have a good attitude towards money and should have some money. To appreciate the value of money, we should not look at what it can't do, but at what it does. Those who say that money can't buy health, for example, should try to fill their trolley with goods at a grocery store and tell the cashier that they will buy the groceries with their health. My guess is the cashier will either call the police, or send them to a mental hospital.

Everyone should learn how to make, spend, employ money and give away. You need to know how much of your Rand (South African currency) you need to spend, keep, give away, and employ. Spending has to do with what you use to get stuff. What you employ has to do with how much you use to multiply your money. Just as critical is knowing how much you need to give away.

There are two ways of earning money. One is called wages and the other is called profit. Wages are what you are given for working for someone, and profit is what you get for adding value. Even when you work for someone, when you are using the profit paradigm, you don't look at yourself as an employee but someone who is adding value and getting paid for it. People who only have a wages paradigm don't improve themselves to improve on their craft because they depend on others to give them money for selling their time. People who are profit-oriented, even when they are working for someone, put more into their work knowing that it is about value, not just selling time. Eventually, the profit-oriented people will end up getting rich because sometimes they start their own businesses or end up climbing the corporate ladder. Their aim is to give value, not to just sell time.

Hobbies Sphere

"And out of the ground Jehovah God caused to grow every tree that is pleasant to the sight, and good for food"[15].

When God created trees in the Garden of Eden, which was the first habitation of man, He did not just create trees that were good for food. He created others that were just good to look at. Aesthetics are part of who we are. To get wowed is part of the human experience and when we don't deliberately pursue our hobbies to get wowed, we are suppressing something that is as human as the other six things.

God created a human being with an imagination. A human is the only one of God's creatures that can look at the sunset and get wowed. The wow comes from a deeper place in our humanness and we don't have to feel that that is not important.

Therefore, to have a complete, whole life, we need to pursue our hobbies. To be complete we need to deliberately go after those things that interest us. Entertainment, the arts, and other things like sport,

---

15. Genesis 2:9; Modern King James Version of Bible

are all part of God's creation. We cannot take them outside the human experience and label them unimportant or evil as we usually do. Some people think these are just necessary evils that we have to put up with.

The fact that some entertainment is contaminated with lust and other evils does not make entertainment itself evil. Entertainment is not evil in itself, but can be used to perpetuate an evil agenda.

Balancing on Purpose

1.   What was your biggest lesson(s) in this chapter?

....
....
....
....
....
....
....
....
....
....
....
....

2.   How will you apply them to your life?

....
....
....
....
....
....
....
....
....
....
....

Chapter 2
Your Success Ratio

The world's definition of success usually covers only part of what real success is. Only people with seven healthy cows (spheres) can call themselves successful. However, the world has redefined success. A healthy financial and career life is what is called success in our world today. This is irrespective of what is happening in other aspects of your life.

When we look at God's definition of success, which is defined by the word "Shalom" in Hebrew, we see that His idea of success has to do with completeness. This completeness has to be in all the seven aspects of our human experience.

The word "Shalom," which is usually translated "Peace" in the English language, means "having nothing missing and nothing broken, implying that one has everything they need, are enjoying great relationships with family and friends and are also healthy in the body". It means to have all-around success. Using our metaphor of the cows, we would say that success means having seven healthy cows.

"The LORD Almighty, the God of Israel, says to all those people whom he allowed Nebuchadnezzar to take away as prisoners from Jerusalem to Babylonia: 'Build houses and settle down. Plant gardens and eat what you grow in them. Marry and have children. Then let your children get married, so that they also may have children. You must increase in numbers and not decrease. Work for the good of the cities where I have made you go as prisoners. Pray to me on their behalf, because if they are prosperous, you will be prosperous too... I alone know the plans I have for you, plans to bring you prosperity and not disaster, plans to bring about the future you hope for".[16]

To God, prosperity is not in half measures. He does not consider someone prosperous who has a lot of success in one or two areas and has suffering in other important areas. The scripture we quoted above shows us that prosperity is wholeness, not just having

---

16. Jeremiah 29:4-11; Good News Bible; E-Sword

a few areas covered. We see that it touched such things as marriage, children, business/career, being happy and prayer. While the scripture may not have mentioned all the seven spheres directly, all of them have been implied.

Most people pursue career and financial success at the expense of their families, relationships and health. Career or business and financial success are just part of the bigger picture. These in isolation from the other five do not constitute success. These are part of a whole and when they are taken in isolation, it is not different from someone who would say that just because they are healthy and have a great family it means they are successful.

Our success ratio sometimes becomes a confusing matter because we consider people to be successful if they are successful in the two mentioned areas. We do not consider people to be successful if they are not doing well in their careers and financial lives. However, to calculate one's success ratio, one should not just consider two things. One should calculate it from all the seven areas.

I have included a quiz at the end of this book that you can take to calculate your real success ratio. At this moment in the book you understand the seven spheres (cows), the quiz will help you to see how you are doing in each sphere and will calculate your real success ratio. Please go to the quiz and finish it to calculate your success ratio.

Quiz

There are 5 questions for each sphere of life in the quiz, and each question has a score of 1 to 5. 1 means you are no doing that and 5 means you are doing it. This means that each sphere has a score of up to 25, and having 7 spheres, the total score can be as high as 175. When you have found your total score, find the percentage thereof out of 175. The percentage is your real success ratio.

Your Success Ratio Formula

Your total score X 100 divided by 175 = Your success ratio

Record below and see how successful you are.

1. Health =
2. Spirituality =
3. Family =
4. Relationships =
5. Hobbies =
6. Career =
7. Financial =

Total Score: _________________ X 100 / 175

My Success Ratio is: _________________________

FAT and THIN Cows

As you do your quiz, something important to remember is that just like the story of the cows in Genesis 41, a high score in a few areas is eaten up by the lower-score areas. This is true in arithmetic as it is in our real lives. We should be careful that we do not look at success in isolation of other areas.

Someone may say, wait a minute. Who in this time and age would have all the seven cows healthy? It is not possible to have all the cows fed, one has to sacrifice to be successful, so you say. As a matter of fact, I read a book where the writer says that it is impossible to be rich if you don't sacrifice your family life. He said that if you want to be rich you need to be prepared to have a bad marriage, a terrible family, and sometimes even ready to divorce a few times. He himself has done that several times it seems.

This is a lie from the enemy. To be rich should not be the goal of our lives at the expense of other things like family, relationships, health, etc. We need to be rich and healthy and spiritual and have great families and great friends too. This view that to be rich you need to sacrifice other important areas of your life is erroneous and does not support God's perspective.

Balancing on Purpose

1.   What was your biggest lesson(s) in this chapter?

....
....
....
....
....
....
....
....
....
....
....
....

2.   How will you apply them to your life?

....
....
....
....
....
....
....
....
....
....
....
....

Chapter 3
The Knock-On Effect

"He who digs a pit shall fall into it; and whoever breaks a hedge, a snake shall bite him"[17].

Life is like a chain; it is as strong as its weakest link. If every link but one is strong, your chain will break under pressure at its weak point and will drop everything that is held by that chain. Your life is the same: if you leave some areas unattended, and only look after others, the ones that are neglected will cause havoc, not only in one, but in all of your life. You can't say that, because you are healthy, it is fine to be broke. Or say that because you are rich, you need to neglect your health, and your relationships are not that important. You need both health and wealth, and you need great relationships too.

When the Lord started giving me insight into the integration of the seven spheres of life. It started dawning on me how easy it is for our lives to get into

---

17. Ecclessiastes 10:8, Good News Bible

a tailspin because we have neglected an area of our lives that we probably took for granted.

One of the things that is shocking is how we tend to compartmentalize our lives. We live our lives in boxes. The danger of doing so is that we see other boxes as important and others as semi-important. Some are just tolerated or even neglected, but others get our full attention.

This way of looking at life and living life is so dangerous that most of the pain we go through comes from this same attitude. It is easy to go off on a tangent and just pick two or three areas and run with them, and completely neglect the others. Unfortunately, even if they seem neglected, the truth is that they are not left parked somewhere. They are still part of who you are. They are still with you and in one way or the other they will demand your attention. You are better off deliberately giving them attention, instead of them demanding it.

When I took some introspection of my own life, it was clear that I had fallen victim to this way of living, especially during my first pastorate. I was one of those that took off with family, spirituality, and relationships at the expense of my finances, health, and hobbies. I loved my wife. I had great friends who sometimes went out of their way to try to help me when I had been felled with a tragedy, like the loss of my dad for example. I made sure that I kept my spiritual disciplines like prayer, reading God's word, and fellowship with other believers alive. I was all in on my career as a pastor.

On the other hand, I had completely neglected my financial life. I earned little to nothing. My salary as a pastor was less than my rent–not that I was living in a mansion; no, I was living in a two-bedroom flat. I lied to myself that God was going to provide the deficit because I was a good man. It turned out God expected me to grow up and take care of my responsibility of getting my financial life in order. I needed to increase my earning capacity.

It was not long that lack of finances started to interfere with my other areas. Because my wife had to carry most of the financial load, she started to feel the weight. Fights about money were not uncommon in our house. I started to borrow money from friends to patch up our situation. This started eating my relationships because I was not earning enough; I had no money to pay back my friends. Relationships started getting strained. My health and that of my wife started to be affected. In 2007 my wife had a stroke due to a burst vein in her brain. It was clear that pressure had gotten to her. I developed ulcers and lived in constant abdominal pain. Something had to be done because my other cows were ravaging the ones that I had concentrated on. It was clear that if I didn't take control of this situation, my health was going to eat up even the little money I was earning and perhaps kill my career due to ill health.

I am not documenting this because I want to show you how much suffering I went through. I am documenting this to show you what happens when you neglect other aspects of your life. Because these areas are integrated, those that are neglected will start to eat the ones that are healthy. Some balance must be achieved. If you don't do it intentionally, life itself will force the balance. With me it was the finances that started to eat my marriage, and my relationships, and my health. For others it is their relationships that start to eat their finances, etc. Unfortunately when the thin cows eat up the fat ones, they don't get fat themselves.

"The thin cows ate up the fat ones, but no one would have known it, because they looked just as bad as before."[18]

As humans, we live in different dimensions. However, these dimensions don't exist as separate entities but as one whole. That is why, when one part is ailing, the whole crumbles. You can easily be fooled to think that when one part (which is part of the whole) is doing badly, other areas that are not doing badly themselves won't be affected. That is the biggest lie from the enemy.

Paul in his letters to the Corinthians made it very plain that a body is one whole and if part of it is in trouble, the whole body is in trouble. That is a good metaphor of what happens in our own lives. When we neglected other aspects of it, the whole gets affected.

"For as the body is one, and hath many members, and all the members of that one body, being many, are one body: so also is Christ"[19]

As I was doing some introspection, I took the liberty of looking at some other people's lives. I

---

[18] Genesis 41:20-21; Good News Bible.
19. 1 Corinthians 12:12; King James Version of the Bible; E-Sword

noticed that some people I knew had very "successful" careers but had certain areas of their lives really in trouble. Others had financial issues sorted but had other areas like relationships or marriages in big trouble.

As I examined what the Lord was showing me, a pattern started to form. I saw that every time someone concentrated on nurturing one or two, or even three, areas of their lives, those areas that they concentrated on started to suffer because of the areas they neglected. I knew people whose careers were in trouble because of marital problems. They had concentrated on developing their business or career and neglected their marriage. Now the marriage was eating up the very thing they concentrated on.

Don't take me wrong. I also saw a few lives that were well-balanced. These people had a plan in place to balance their lives. Their lives were balanced on purpose. Nonetheless, they were very few. Both in church and in business, I saw very few people that had it all together.

The knock-on effect that we are speaking about is so critical that if a person decides to ignore the "cow" that is being eaten, chances are that all his or her cows will at some point become thin. This is where you find a person who was seemingly doing well financially loses it all. They start to drink hard or use other substances as a crutch to suppress the pain. Some seemingly normal people have ended up doing drastic things like committing suicide and people were shocked.

I used to get shocked, but not anymore, when such a thing happens. With this knowledge I am able to understand that something in their lives was in very bad shape and started to interfere with other things to such an extent that taking their own life seemed the only option. Nonetheless, the truth is that killing themselves was not the only option; there are other options. Balancing one's life intentionally will eventually stop the vicious cycle.

Balancing on Purpose

1.   What was your biggest lesson(s) in this chapter?

....

....

....

....

....

....

....

....

....

....

....

2.   How will you apply them to your life?

....

....

....

....

....

....

....

....

....

....

....

Chapter 4
Pain: Identifying an Angry Cow

Pain acts as a signal that something is not right in one or more spheres of your life. Pain is a signal to you so you can pay attention. When we suffer pain our natural tendency is to eradicate the pain by rescuing the cow that is being eaten, instead of feeding the one that is eating the other. When our health cow is being eaten, we spend all our money trying to get our health back. My question is, what if you also spent some money on improving some areas that you have neglected. What if sickness was a signal that you are not resting enough, or that you are not eating well because you are always on the run and not spending any time watching what you eat?

This is what I have found out since I started to apply this knowledge to my life. When solving a problem in any area of your life, *don't* just fix the area where you have a problem, if it is bad shape, fix it but look into other spheres and see what is happening there. There could be a thin cow that is eating your other cow. Most of the time the problem is another area. The fact that you are sick usually doesn't mean that if you get chemicals to heal yourself you will be fine. The symptoms will be gone, and yes you can get healed, but you may not be made whole. Wholeness comes when you eradicate what made you sick in the first place, if the sickness was due to an area that you neglected.

Go to the root cause and not the symptom. The root cause, the cow that is eating your health sphere, needs to be addressed–otherwise it will not only eat your health, when it's done with your health it will target another cow. There are times you have to resuscitate the cow because it is almost dead, but after that, look into other areas. Leave the attacked cow alone. It is not your problem. The one eating it is the problem.

In the previous chapter we looked at how our lives are a whole, not a sum total, of seven areas. The seven areas, though distinct, all make up one whole life. This means that what is happening in one area affects the other areas. The negative effect happening in one area is a negative in the whole. A positive happening in one area is a positive happening in all.

In this chapter, I want to help you see a flaw in our problem-solving approach. I was stunned by what I saw as a common pattern in how we solve our problems. I clearly saw why our problems don't get solved. We think we are solving a problem, not knowing that we are just trying to numb a symptom.

As an example, when we have a money problem, we usually go all out to go look for money. When we have a marital problem, we go for counseling to get our marriage on track. This is the default problem-solving approach. It is like rescuing the cow that is being eaten is our natural tendency. This may look right but it is not in most cases.

While this approach may relieve the symptoms, it leaves the main problem unattended. What I discovered from the metaphor of the seven cows is that when a cow is being eaten, you don't need to rescue it. What you need to do is identify the cow that is eating the cow that's in trouble. By identifying an angry cow, you are in effect rescuing the fat cow that is being eaten. By just trying to rescue the cow that is being eaten and leaving the other as hungry as it was, you are not solving the problem.

I will give you a practical example in my own life. When I noticed that my life was in a tailspin, it was my marriage, my relationships, and my health that were in trouble. Naturally, I wanted to go for counseling, and as a matter of fact my wife and I discussed this many times. To get my health back, I was taking a lot of over-the-counter antacid medicines because I couldn't afford a hospital consultation, let alone going to do a thorough checkup. The idea of going to a government hospital made me even sicker.

I am sure you are thinking, is this not what every person with a brain would do? Wrong! That is what our default setting will tell us to do but that setting is faulty. That is why it is a de-"fault" setting. It is faulty! I don't think it came faulty; we just set it wrongly ourselves. I am sure that God didn't put it that way.

In my case, I was blessed because, in my distress, I sat down with my Bible, and God through His word started pouring this revelation into me. I was able to see that if I just went for counseling, or tried to mend my relationships and go to have my ulcer operated on or whatever they would do to it, it was not going to solve my real problem. My problem was not a bad marriage, or bad relationships, or ill health. Yes that is what I was experiencing and I needed to have those things sorted. However, my real problem was lack of money. I was not earning enough money to look after my family and that was causing stress in the family, and it was having a negative effect on my marriage. I had also borrowed money from almost every one of my friends because the bank couldn't lend me money due to my lack of earning capacity. I came to learn that high levels of stress can cause all kinds of medical conditions and ulcers are on the list.

When I got a handle on what my real problem was, I went to work on the real issue. The first thing I did was to resign from my job as a pastor. I started a consulting business to increase my earning capacity. As my earning power went up, and started to relieve the financial pressure that my family was going through, many things started to fall into place. The pressure in the marriage is long gone and I can see how even my health is responding. All this because I identified the cow that was causing havoc. I have paid back almost everyone their money and my relationships are better than they used to be.

Don't rescue the cow; doing that does not bring a lasting solution. The lasting solution lies in your identifying the cow that has been eating your other cows. When you do that, start to deliberately feed it, or them if they are more than one, so that they can also start to get healthy. Remember how in the past chapter we discussed integration of these aspects of our lives. What happens negatively when some parts of the whole are having problems, also happens positively when you start to feed the starving cows.

You could be reading this book and wondering why certain areas of your life are in such turmoil. Don't focus there. It is very rare that where you are feeling the pain is the cause of your pain. Many times the real cause of pain is somewhere else. If you take some time to examine your life, you will discover that what you thought was your problem is actually the only thing that is going well in your life.

Some people have divorced thinking that they no longer love their wife or husband. What they didn't know is that it was not their spouse that was the problem. It could be that they neglected the relationship due to work, or other reasons. There are those who could even be going through some ill health and thinking that they need to drink some chemical-based medication. What they may not realize is that if they can focus on hobbies that they have neglected their health will improve.

These things are so simple but they are critical to our wholeness. Wholeness is different from the sum of many things. When you add things together, they maintain their personal identity. When you fuse them together to make a whole, they become one new thing made up of many things.

We are not a sum of seven dimensions. We are a whole made of seven dimensions. If you can get that, you will respect all aspects of your life and keep yourself from the pain I see in many people's lives.

1. What was your biggest lesson(s) in this chapter?

....
....
....
....
....
....
....
....
....
....
....
....

2. How will you apply them to your life?

....
....
....
....
....
....
....
....
....
....
....
....

Chapter 5
Sources of Values and Beliefs

When something is not dealt with at the root, all you can do is treat symptoms. Many experts say that the cause of many diseases is our wrong thought patterns which trigger negative emotions. The negative emotions are said to produce chemical imbalances in our bodies and cause sicknesses. Therefore, to try to cure a disease and leave the wrong thought pattern is to cure symptoms and leave the root intact. Chances are, the disease will re-occur.

In the same way, the cause of most pain in our lives is wrong values. The wrong values influence the way we look at life and end up producing wrong sets of beliefs. These wrong beliefs produce chaos in our lives. To really change our lives, we need to change our values and our beliefs.

Most of how we live is as a result of what we think is important. The way the world operates, and the message popular culture is sending to us daily is that success is money, and possessions. Family, relationships, health, and such other important areas of our lives are low on our scale of important things. This is the cause of most problems we face.

Society through many mediums bombards us with these values and create a set of beliefs that are wrong. Our beliefs come from three levels of conditioning. We become conditioned by verbal information from the things that we hear often and internalise. We also get our beliefs from modelling by seeing other people which may include authority figures like parents, teachers, and those people we admire. Thirdly, we get indoctrinated through our own experiences as we interact with life and we form conclusions about how the world is. Most of the times our conclusions are not based on reality, and are wrong.

Our worldly system has values and beliefs that are anti-life. They promote things that cause problems in our lives. Unfortunately, most people have no sense to go counter culture and live according to what God wants us to live. We take everything we see and hear from all the worldly sources of values as gospel truth. In the end we get our other cows so thin that they eat up everything and take us to an early grave.

Let me list a few areas that pass on these wrong values to us.

Parents

Parents are responsible for most of the beliefs which eventually become values in our lives. These beliefs are unknowingly passed on to children. They are passed on through attitudes, the words they speak, and the way they interact with their children. Children see their parents' attitudes towards the seven dimensions of life and end up forming beliefs about each one of these areas. That is why families usually have similar values, until one realises that some may be flawed and change them intentionally. Something that is easy to say, but very difficult to do.

Children who grow up seeing parents trivialise certain aspects of life and venerate others adopt the same attitude and end up having the same attitude towards life. They end up looking at other aspects of life as important and others as trivial, just as they saw their parents do. The culture or beliefs passed on to children from parents form a foundation for what they will believe to be right or wrong about life.

For example, if parents are very religious, and they trivialise the importance of money as most religious people do, children grow up thinking that money is not that important. Some even think money is evil. Such people only consider as important such things as their spirituality and relationships and the rest of other dimensions of our human experience as trivia.

Sometimes parents may not speak directly about a value they espouse about an area of life but will model before their children what is important and what is not. Children pick up their parents' values as they observe them living them out. As they see them live out those values, the children also adopt the same values.

Society or Socialisation

Socialisation works the same way as parenting, except that it happens on a broader scale. When one grows up in a society that values relationships highly, they will value relationships over such things as career or money. To them, career, business, or money will be things they look at as necessary evils–things that are necessary but not that important.

Just as it happens in a family setup, the same happens in the society through many channels like television and school. People pick up these values as they interact with other people in a society. Every society has its own values and has avenues through which these values are communicated.

Most of what is shown on television, for example, is seen as the ideal life for most people. The values shown in the movies and other TV shows constantly communicate values to the people that watch. As we watch those things on television we adopt the values portrayed in the shows. The messages sent through these mediums have specific values about each of the seven areas of life.

For example, most TV shows have a very loose attitude towards premarital and extramarital sex. Do you wonder why many people may not have a strong stance about sex outside marriage? Where did they get that value from? How did it get to them?

When it comes to success, society has its own outlook on what success is. Usually career, business, and financial well-being is looked at as success. Other things, like relationships and marriage and spirituality, are disposable. They are not seen to be as important as the other three. A person who has money but has a terrible marriage is still looked at as successful in most societies.

Therefore, to adopt values that will look at all the seven areas of life as important takes a lot of deliberately unlearning what society has taught us. There are powerful TV personalities who have publicly attacked marriage and many people have been influenced. There are powerful personalities that have trivialised the importance of a spiritual life and belief in a personal God and most people have been attacked by that venom. Society portrays having lots of money and possessions as the only form of success. Be careful about what society pushes at you. You may not know why certain areas of your life are in trouble; it may just be that you haven't adopted the right values.

Many people have testified that after having all the money and possessions, they realised that there is more to life. They realised that having all the money and possessions without their children to enjoy it with was vain. Some have spent their lives pursuing financial success only to pay it all to a hospital due to ill health. Success is having seven cows not two.

Religion

Most religions venerate a life of poverty because they look at this life not to be as important as the afterlife. In most religions, people are considered highly spiritual when they live lives of poverty. We hear of monks who live in mountains with just a bowl to use for eating and a simple tunic as clothing. These people are considered highly spiritual and their followers look up to them as noble men. They become role models to everyone in those particular religions.

This creates a psychological hatred for other human experiences like pursuing hobbies, or financial and career success. Many religions also consider this world as fallen, and all that is happening in it to be evil, which causes them to treat this life with disdain. Yes, the worldly systems that are running the world are fallen, but God's world is just fine. This makes most people in these religions look at their spiritual life as more important than other dimensions of their life. You may not be an extremist, but if you dig deeper, you may just find some traces of these attitudes towards the world in you, if your religious affiliation is pushing this agenda.

I have nothing against religion; I am a devout Christian myself, a pastor for that matter. However, I know that religion is responsible for some of the pain people go through because it teaches and models that some dimensions of our human experience are evil, and others are just to be tolerated. What we need to teach people is that there are some ways of expressing our human experience that are evil, not that this whole life is sinful. That is why most religious people cannot conceive the thought that God is delighted when they are out expressing their hobbies.

One of the areas where religion has caused a lot of havoc is its erroneous teaching about financial success. Some religions are on one end, teaching that poverty is punishment from God, while others teach that financial success is of the devil. Both these extremes are erroneous. What we need to know is that financial success is one of the seven dimensions in which we as humans live. We should not look at it as more important or as less important than the other dimensions of our human experience. It is just as important as the other six. We need to have a healthy desire to be financially independent. We need to pursue legitimate and legal ways of achieving financial independence. There is nothing wrong in that.

Government

There are times when governments make laws that send wrong messages and model wrong values to the people. The constitution of a government, for example, is a reflection of the values that that particular government upholds. When a nation's constitution allows pornography, abortion, and other values that are against Biblical principles, people adopt that as their value system.

The power of the government is such that the school system also adopts what the government considers as the right values in their teaching of its children. As in the case of evolution versus creation, most government schools teach evolution as the true account of how this world was made. The world is said to have developed from lesser forms of life and finally ended up with what is there today. The problem is that, up to now, there are still traces of society that believe that certain groups of people (for example) are not fully evolved. This is the root of most racial hatred and cultural biases that we see in our societies. All these are values that are put forward by wrong understanding of the world.

While we are all expected by God to obey the government that is in place. It is not wrong to question certain things that may go against your personal value system and to form a value system that will serve you. Governments are necessary, but because they are led by fallen people like all of us, they are not perfect. That is why we need to be careful about some of the things that may even find their way into the constitution. It is not all of them that send the right message nor model the best values.

Common Beliefs

I want to take some liberty and delve into some common values that influence people. Remember that your value system will always play a major role in determining which of the seven areas you will pick as most important and which ones will be neglected. Your values determine how you view each of the seven areas that we have continuously been talking about in this book.

In his book to the Romans, Paul cautioned them that they should watch out for the values that society was imposing on them. These values are not always good for us. Society is corrupt and for us to get clear of its fallenness, we need to take a high road. The world has its own values concerning each of the seven areas and it is up to us to choose which ones are in line with God's word and which ones should be discarded.

Spirituality

This is what Paul said to the Romans:

"And do not be conformed to this world, but be transformed by the renewing of your mind, in order to prove by you what is that good and pleasing and perfect will of God".[20]

In the area of spirituality, what causes a lot of people's spiritual cow to get eaten is the wrong belief that spirituality equals religion. Nothing can be further from the truth. Religion and spirituality are two different things. Our Savior Jesus was not religious but He was spiritual. He never came to start a religion but a life that had spiritual harmony. Alan

---

20. Romans 12:2; Modern King James Version of the Bible; E-Sword

Platt, who has become a big influence in my grace theology usually says; "That Jesus was not an example for us but of us". Jesus was not showing us what we should constantly strive to become, but to live out what we became through Him. He came to give an example that it was possible to live a life that is in harmony with our Father's will and through Him we have access to that. He was not an example of what we can be; He was an example of what we are.

Jesus did not come to make human beings superhumans. He came to show us what it was to be human. A life with Christ is a revelation of what being a real human is all about. A life without Him is a lesser life because we cannot reach our full potential as humans without being alive to our spiritual potential. Our spirituality, as Christ showed us through His own life, and now through us believing in what He purchased for us through His death, allows us to be fully human.

Because people hate religion, most of them lose out on a great life because they think spirituality and religion are the same thing. As a result of this wrong view, people don't take care of their spiritual cow and it starts to eat other cows. Your spirituality is so important that, if it is out of whack, a lot of things in your life can go wrong. Because we are more than just physical, we need to also take care of our spiritual side of life. Our spirituality has got nothing to do with religion, but everything to do with our being in touch with our spiritual side, and Christ provides both a way and an example of how.

Beliefs That Wreck Our Physical Bodies

While every one of us knows the importance of having a healthy and fit body, we don't take this seriously because we think that keeping ourselves healthy and fit is just a necessity but not that important. Wrong! Keeping our bodies healthy and fit is as important as pursuing a career to feed our families. If you are one of those people who think that God does not care about how you treat your body, think again.

Our wrong belief that keeping our bodies in tip-top condition is not that important is the cause for most of our problems. When these bodies get sick, they start to cause havoc in other areas of our life. A sick body can't work, as a result can't earn, and when you are not earning a lot of things can go wrong. I don't even need to list what can go wrong when we are sick. One of the areas that is easily attacked by ill health is our finances.

Someone once said that there are people who work so hard that they make themselves sick and spend all the money they worked hard for to try to get well. I think God does not want us to work ourselves sick. He wants us to have a good balance so that we can enjoy our money.

Family, Marriage and Other Relationship Beliefs

A common belief about relationships is that our loved ones will understand that we are busy. This belief manifests itself in how people take their loved ones for granted. Most people will put their career, business, and many other things above their family. While again I am not advocating an extreme which puts family ahead of everything, my approach is to look at all these areas as important. They are not a hierarchy, but a blend of many things making up one whole.

We make a mistake when we put these seven areas in a hierarchy. A hierarchy puts things in order of importance, which means some areas find themselves at the top while others are at the bottom. This is a wrong way of looking at life. The right way is to see every area as important and give each the right amount of attention.

Most relationships, be it in marriage, or friendships fail because the people in them take each other for granted. They put other things above relationships. They work hard at work at the expense of relationships. They neglect their children and other family members in order to pursue other cows. We don't take intentional time and effort to nurture our relationships the way we do with other areas of our lives. One of my favorite songs was done by Billy Cyrus and its called Busy Man. In the song he talks how we neglect our families in pursuit of work. Great song to learn from.

Hobbies

Most people don't believe that hobbies are an important part of our lives. We usually say that when our financial situation gets better, then we can indulge in our hobbies. That is quoting trouble.

When you ignore your hobbies, in one way or another they will eat up one of the areas of your life and force you to slow down. Some people have been known to completely have a nervous breakdown after working continuously, without rest to focus on their hobbies, and were forced to rest. Hobbies are a great way of replenishing your energies so that you can do other things optimally. Hobbies may not require the same time to be nurtured as others areas, but they are just as important as any other area.

Career and Money

The areas that have the most wrong beliefs are those of career and money. The world defines success as doing well in these two areas. These two areas don't make up success; they are part of a bigger picture.

However, some people may say money is not everything, which is true, but they should not take that to mean it is nothing. Money, which is usually a spinoff of a successful career or business, is often misunderstood. I agree that money is not everything, but to say it is nothing is just as wrong. Someone once said that "Money is power, and you ought to be reasonably ambitious to have it". I agree a hundred percent. Nonetheless, if money is in isolation from the other six things, it does not constitute success. It is like saying that, if I am really healthy, it means I have everything. If I don't have money but have health, it won't be long until I will be unhealthy because hunger will make sure I am. Health does not buy groceries at the supermarket. Health does not pay school fees. Health is good when it is looked at as part of the seven dimensions, not in isolation.

All the Seven Cows Should Be Fed

Any of the seven areas is not enough when it stand alone. There is not one of these areas which can stand alone and the person will be okay. Christians confuse a scripture which says "man can't live by bread alone" to mean that the spiritual side of things is more important.

"He made you go hungry, and then he gave you manna to eat, food that you and your ancestors had never eaten before. He did this to teach you that you must not depend on bread alone to sustain you, but on everything that the LORD says".[21]

---

21. Deuteronomy 8:2; Good News Bible; E-Sword.

This scripture is very clear but we refuse to see what it says deliberately. This scripture plainly says man needs both the spiritual and the physical for his sustenance. The two are not in a hierarchy; they are equally important. The word "alone" suggests that he needs both. He does not need just the physical alone, neither does he need the spiritual alone, but both.

These few common beliefs that I have highlighted, and many more that you can add to the list, are causing havoc in our lives. What we need to constantly do is to evaluate whether our beliefs are working for us or against us. Are they causing other cows to get malnourished and others fat, or are we living a balanced life?

Balancing on Purpose

1. What was your biggest lesson(s) in this chapter?

....
....
....
....
....
....
....
....
....
....
....

2. How will you apply them to your life?

....
....
....
....
....
....
....
....
....
....
....
....

Chapter 6
Defining Your Own Success

We attribute importance to particular cows because of the way we define success. What we think is important and what we think has value determines what we think is success. We already saw how different sources influence what we value.

What Is Success?

When you take a simple survey to ask people what success is, you will probably find that 80 to 90 percent of the people will define success in terms of what someone has. Very few people will define success in terms of what someone has become, or who they are as a person. I have to yet find a definition of success that incorporates both what someone has and who they are as a person. Actually, as a matter of fact, some people believe that you can't be both successful and a good person at the same time. Success and being 'nice' does not mix so they say.

Our definition of success will influence which of the seven spheres of our lives will be given priority. When we view success as having things, and not as including who we are as a person, our whole lives will be preoccupied with activities that have to do with the accumulation of things. While we may have families and friends, we will not deliberately take time to nurture our relationships. We will do so when it is convenient, but not deliberately.

One of the most debilitating cancers that our society has is our fear of missing out. While we may know that success includes more than just what we have, most people are terrified to model that. They would rather live someone else's definition of success than what they know success is. Other people may know and even want to live their own definition of success but for lack of guts to stand their ground, they live someone else's definition.

To avert living someone else's script of what success is, it is imperative that one defines and lives one's own definition of success. Success is different for everyone but it should always include health in all the seven spheres of life. If success only include a few of the seven spheres, it doesn't really matter who said that or who defines it that way–that is not success at all.

A healthy balance in all the seven spheres of life is what real success entails. If you are afraid of what people will say, or how they will look at you when you define your own success, chances are you are going to get yourself into a painful experience because your cows will start eating each other. Define your own success and stop living someone else's definition.

What Is Important?

What we consider important in our lives will always influence how we live our lives. Our schedule will be filled with things we consider important. Our time will be given to things we consider important. Our money will be spent on things we consider important. Our lives are a sum total of what we consider important.

Unfortunately, very few people determine for themselves what is important. Most people follow what the larger society is dictating as what is important. Even when they know that to be not true, for fear of standing out, they adopt what the broader society says.

What Are Your Values?

The danger of following the broader society without consideration is that because, our societies are fallen, we will always follow the wrong path. What television and the mainstream media puts out there as important may not really be what is important. At the most, if they put out what is important, it is usually aspects of the truth and not the whole truth.

If what is important does not include all the seven spheres, that is not the whole truth. If what is important denigrates any of the other spheres of life, that is misleading. If you want to spare yourself from pain, consider looking at every one of the seven spheres as important. Others are not more important than the others. They are all the same and all should be accorded same importance.

Balancing on Purpose

1. What was your biggest lesson(s) in this chapter?

....
....
....
....
....
....
....
....
....
....
....
....

2. How will you apply them to your life?

....
....
....
....
....
....
....
....
....
....
....
....

Chapter 7
Living In Babylon

In this chapter, I want to show how our societies have become a replica of the Babylonian system that was instituted thousands of years ago. In the book of Genesis, the Bible shows us a society in a place called Shinar. This society was said to be involved in a project that God Himself had to stop. Most people don't have a clear picture of why God stopped this project.

There were three things within this society that compelled God to stop this project. The story is found in Genesis chapter 11. For context's sake, I would like to quote this passage before I start to deal with the three reasons why God stopped this project.

"And the whole earth was of one language and of one speech. And it happened, as they traveled from the east, they found a plain in the land of Shinar. And they lived there. And they said to one another, Come, let us make brick and burn them

thoroughly. And they had brick for stone, and they had asphalt for mortar. And they said, Come, let us build us a city and a tower, and its top in the heavens. And let us make a name for ourselves, lest we be scattered upon the face of the whole earth. And Jehovah came down to see the city and the tower which the sons of Adam had built".[22]

Reason Number 1: Building With Brick Instead of Stone

The passage emphasizes the fact that this project was done by brick and not stone. While it may look innocent to the untrained eye that the Bible emphasizes the material that the people used to build their city, the material they used to build was one of the reasons why God stopped this project. Building using stone reveal an attitude that led God to stop the project.

Building with stone is a totally different process from building using bricks. There are two important factors about building with stone. The first is that stones maintain their uniqueness while they

---

22

Genesis 11:1-5; Modern King James Version Bible

are part of the whole. They have to find a fit within the building process, while the bricks can fit anywhere and they all look the same.

God wants every human to maintain their uniqueness within the building. God has a unique purpose for everyone and have a place to fit into a society where He has placed them. Any system that diminishes our uniqueness is evil. Most societies discourage human uniqueness. When people fail to acknowledge or when they are forced by a system to despise their uniqueness, they tend to diminish their potential.

"From one human being he created all races of people and made them live throughout the whole earth. He himself fixed beforehand the exact times and the limits of the places where they would live."[23]

When Nimrod built the city using brick, he was displaying a very evil system that is prevalent in many societies. Most societies treat people like "masses" and don't encourage individuality. This is a problem because, for people to perform at their

---

[23]. Acts 17:26; Good News Bible

optimum, they need to maintain their individual uniqueness.

Secondly, building with brick reveals the need for control. Man is obsessed with control, either of fellow man or other things. When it comes to controlling other humans, man usually kills the unique identity of an individual to classify them by race, tribe, what they do, where they come from, etc. This is evident in bricks; they are usually identical and of the same colour. It is easy to build with them all you need is pile them one on top of the other. As of stone, you need to find a place to fit it. Another very important thing to note is that there are no off-cuts with stones. Because every stone has a unique shape, it cannot be an off-cut. The builder just needs to find a place to fit even the funniest shaped stone. It is not so with bricks. If it is out of shape or broken, the builder throws it away or uses it for lesser important purposes. God wants us to respect our unique identity as individuals because that is what makes us different from animals.

Reason Number 2:

The Tower in the Middle of the City

"And they said, Come, let us build us a city and a tower, and its top in the heavens".[24]

In this passage, we are given an impression that the tower these people were building was so tall that the top would reach God in Heaven. However, the right understanding of this scripture is simply that the tower was used as a place where people could reach Heaven, or rather interact with their spirituality. They separated God from their human activities such as marriage, business, family, hobbies, and careers and built Him a tower where they would go to meet Him. Does that sound familiar?

It is difficult for people today to build business, education, government, the arts, and entertainment with God. We have separated the spiritual and the physical to our own detriment. The two are part of one whole. Life is a whole made up of spiritual and physical reality. However, the Babylonian agenda has successfully separated the two.

---

24. Genesis 11:4; Modern King James Version Bible

The material they used revealed to us their attitude towards the uniqueness of an individual. The tower in the middle of the city is showing us that these people only wanted God at a distance, not "meddling" with their everyday lives.

These people had removed God from their day-to-day lives and now they only had a place where they went to meet Him. The tower was used as a place where people went when they wanted to be in touch with Heaven. I am sure by now you are seeing where I am headed with this and how you adopted the values that separate your so-called "life" from what you call religious stuff.

God has always wanted man to interact with Him on a daily basis in what we do in our day to day lives. Man, on the other hand, has removed God from our day-to-day lives and we have created a place for us to meet with him. The tower was the beginning of religion. Religion does not take God out of the picture. It only removes Him from our city life and takes Him to a tower somewhere while we run our own lives in the city. Religion creates a separate life for God from that of our city. God becomes a stranger from the city and is confined to a tower somewhere. In this case, it was in the middle of the city.

Our modern lives are not different from those of the Babylonians of Nimrod's time. We feel God is not intelligent enough to get involved in the city life, so we confine Him to our tower. It can be a building, a tree, a shrine, a temple, etc. Whatever it may be, the principle behind it is to separate God from our lives. God should be kept at a distance; we will go to Him when we are done with our things; so we say in our minds.

Reason Number 3: A City for Ourselves

The third reason why God disturbed the Babylonian project was the motive. The material revealed the attitude. The tower was a practical manifestation of the attitude. But in the end, scripture reveals the motive for the project. The motive was to create a monument for themselves. They wanted to own the success. They didn't want their success to have "God" written on it. Man wants to take God completely out of the picture so he can take all the credit for life. But truth be told, we didn't create ourselves.

The people of Babylon did not want to associate their success with God. They wanted this project to have their name and their name only. They did not want to acknowledge that God was their source and that, with all they achieved, God was the cause of their success.

This Babylonian attitude towards success is very much alive in our societies today. Most people blame God for their problems, but very few acknowledge Him for their success. People want to own their success, just like the Babylonians of old, but blame Him for every mess in the world today. We don't want to attribute our success to someone else other than ourselves. The truth is that it is all about God; without Him there is no life.

The Babylonian System

These three things that I have mentioned play a major role in the formation of our values. After a few hundred years, we see how this same city, now called Babylon, named after the Tower, will put in place a system to instill these value in the people. In the book of Daniel, we see the Babylonian government take over the school system and the popular culture to instill in people its anti-God values.

This is not different today. All mediums of communication– such as television, multimedia, school systems–are taken by a system that is busy instilling values that are anti-God and are causing people to espouse values that bring much pain and suffering in their lives.

When you pay attention to what is communicated on TV and what is floating around on various media platforms, it is values that do not encourage a well-rounded successful life. Some of the cows are belittled. They are looked at as non-essential, while others are looked at a symbol for success. As a result, the people end up espousing values that are portrayed in the media and on TV.

At this point I want to challenge you to look into your life and do a few things. If you find any of these three things present in your life, chances are, one day some of your cows will start eating each other.

1.   What was your biggest lesson(s) in this chapter?

....
....
....
....
....
....
....
....
....
....
....
....

2.   How will you apply them to your life?

....
....
....
....
....
....
....
....
....
....
....
....

Chapter 8
Setting Life Goals

If you want to achieve anything, you need to set goals. The brain needs to be "told" what to focus on; otherwise it will focus on non-important things.

Our brains are fitted with what is called the reticular activating system (RAS). This is a system that tells our brain what to focus on at every particular moment. If you set goals, they act as a guide for what your brain should focus on. Because the brain is bombarded by millions of stimuli every second, if it had to focus on everything, one would go mad. The RAS is like a filter system that lets everything deemed unimportant go unnoticed while only those things that you tell yourself are important will be noticed.

Therefore, your brain will help you in achieving your goals by filtering out of the environment everything that is not supporting the achieving of your goals. It will help you to notice in your environment anything that is supportive to your goals.

The reticular activating system is what determines what you will see, hear, or feel amongst millions of stimuli. For example, because your brain has been told that your spouse is very important, you can be in a crowd with a lot of people speaking but chances are that if your spouse was also among the many voices, you will be able to hear her voice among hundreds of voices in the room. Another common example is about a car, dress, or shirt that you just bought. You will be shocked that, before you bought it, you never saw many people wearing or driving that particular thing. However, as soon as you get it, all of a sudden the world is full of those cars or dresses or shirts.

The truth is that the car or dress has always been there. However, you never saw them because your brain filtered them out. But now that you have it, your brain has registered it as something important. That is why every time there is a car of your type in the vicinity, your brain notices it.

You might be wondering why I am belaboring the RAS in a chapter that is supposed to be for goal setting. What has the RAS got to do with goal setting? Everything!

When I was introducing the RAS, I mentioned the fact that the RAS is responsible for what you pay attention to. The RAS is like a guard by the door to the building. He or she allows who goes in and who doesn't. The environment has a lot of things that happen at the same time. Our five senses are always being bombarded by millions of stimuli in the environment and if the RAS were not filtering things, what to pay attention to and what not to, we would literally go mad. Therefore, what you tell your brain to be important is what the RAS will allow to get your attention.

Now, when you set goals and write them down, especially if you can do it freehand, you will be sending information to your RAS about what is important. Your RAS will then filter out other things and only leave you to see things that may help you to achieve your goals. Your brain will be able to see in your environment opportunities as well as things that may not be obvious to others.

Have you considered why two people could be looking at the same thing but seeing different things? What differentiates what they see is what is important to them. When you set goals, you are telling your brain what is important. When those goals stir up some emotion in you and send some information to your RAS, you set yourself up to achieve those goals, as opposed to a person who has no goals at all. You activate your brain to prioritize information that is important to achieving your goals.

I encourage you to take advantage of this God given tool to use for achieving goals. Set goals and make sure you from time to time read them aloud to yourself. Sometimes it is even advisable to imagine yourself living your goals. Your brain takes that information and will scan the environment for what could help to make that a reality.

Have you considered why, if you concentrate on seeing something good in someone, you end up finding it? But if you also concentrated on seeing something bad, you also end up finding it. In Philippians Paul instructs us what to think about.

"Finally, brothers and sisters, whatever is true, whatever is noble, whatever is right, whatever is pure, whatever is lovely, whatever is admirable—if anything is excellent or praiseworthy—think about such things"[25].

This scripture shows us that God wants us to preoccupy our minds with great thoughts. This is not just so we can have great fantasies. No. It is because if you keep your mind on great thoughts, your chances of accomplishing great things increase.

At this point you may be wondering why I am going on and on about goals in a book about how to balance up your life? The reason is simple. If you are going to intentionally live a balanced life, you will need to set goals in all the seven spheres of life. Things will not just happen. You need to set goals of what you will do or want to do in each of the seven spheres. Set goals of how you will feed each one of your cows and stipulate how you want every cow to look like.

As you set your goals, it is also important to consider three things. Your goals need to have what someone has called the 3 Ps of goals setting. Your goals should be Positive, Personal, and Possible. I would like us to look at these three components of goals setting in light of setting goals to achieve success in all the seven areas of our lives.

---

[25] Philippians 4:8, New International Version of the Bible

Positive

You should phrase your goals positively so that they can make you feel good about yourself and what you're trying to accomplish. The language in your goals setting should be positive. Use positive language not vague or negative. How you phrase a goal can make a big difference in influencing your brain to achieve the goal. If you say you are sick and tired of being unhappy, chances are you won't be motivated internally to be happy. When you say I am a going to smile at two people every day, your brain has a specific task to do to make happiness happen. Saying that you are sick and tired of being unhappy is in itself a defeating statement.

Personal

Personalize your goals. Don't let friends, the media, or anything else influence your goals setting. Let your own dreams and values influence your goals. Always make your goals your own, not someone else's. It is also important to phrase the goals as if you have already achieved them. For example, if you are setting a financial goal, instead of saying "in two years' time I want to be earning R50 000. It will be more powerful to say, "It is 2019, and I am earning R50 000". This sends information to your brain that this reality is possible.

When you say 'I am sick and tired of my marriage", you are generating a lot of negativity. When you say, "I want a great marriage', already you can feel how life giving that statement is from the first one. Most people set their goals with negative language and they wonder why they are not motivated to achieve them.

Possible

When setting goals, be sure to consider what's possible and within your control. Don't go out on a limb and put your head in the clouds and set goals that you know cannot be achieved. Setting yourself up for failure is definitely the best way to discourage yourself. I am a firm believer in thinking big. However, I am also the first one to admit that an elephant cannot be chewed in one bite. Have big dreams, but tackle them one chewable chunk at a time. Think big but don't set yourself up for failure.

A word of caution. Don't set too many goals that you overwhelm yourself and fail to even start. When setting goals, few is more. You have a better chance of achieving your goals if they are few than if you have a long list that you can't even remember any of them. In my personal life I see that when I set between 1 and 4 goals in an area, I usually achieve them easily. It may be different from you but that is my personal experience.

Balancing on Purpose

1. My spiritual goals are:

a) ....

b) ....

c) ....

2. My Physical (Health) goals are:

   a. ....

   b. ....

   c. ....

3. My family goals are:

   a. ....

   b. ....

   c. ....

4. My Relationships (Friendships) goals are:

   a. ....

   b. ....

   c. ....

5. My career/business goals are:

   a. ....

   b. ....

c.	....

6.	My financial goals are:

  a.	....

  b.	....

  c.	....

7.	My Hobbies goals are:

  a.	....

  b.	....

  c.	....

Chapter 9
How to feed your Cows

By now you are familiar with what we mean when I refer to a "cow" or to "cows". We are talking about the spheres of life that we mentioned as the book was starting. The subtitle of this book is "The Story of Seven Cows" because the whole book is based on a metaphor found in the book of Genesis chapter 41. Using the metaphor, we will now show you how to feed every one of the seven cows so that none is thin enough to start eating the fat ones.

There are a few things to consider when you are putting together a feeding plan for your cows. Here below are those things:

1. Time Vs. Importance

As a point of departure, not every cow needs the same amount of time to feed, but that does not mean the ones that require less time are less important. Less time doesn't mean less important. What every one of us should make up our minds to do is to ask ourselves what investment of time it will take to feed every one of the seven spheres. Just because they don't require the same time doesn't mean they are not the same in importance.

Let me also mention that as your life circumstances and age change, the time you spend in these spheres may change. However, the importance remains the same. For example, if you have children, as they grow, you may not require the same time with them as you will need when they are young. However, this should not make you feel that just because now you require less time with your children it means that area of your life is less important. The relationship with your children is still important but may just require less time than it did when the kids where young.

2. Standard of Living Vs. Quality of Life

What gets most people into trouble is their ignorance about the difference between standard of living and quality of life. While quality of life and standard of living are sometimes the same thing, quality of life can sometimes have nothing to do with standard of living. Standard of living is usually what people see while quality of life is what you feel and experience. Some people portray to the outside world something totally different from what they feel.

A person who is obsessed with standard of living chases after things and the outward appearance of life is more important to them. They will do everything to get the latest car, the biggest house in their street; they will get six credit cards to feed their lifestyle and appear to people that they have a higher standard of living, but their quality of life may not be as good. A person who is only looking at standard of living may be doing all these things at the expense of their health, their family, and their relationships. What matters to them is to be seen as living the high life.

On the other hand, people who understand that life is all about quality, not standard alone, will make sure that they nurture all other spheres (feed all the cows) of their lives, and may appear to the outside world as people who are not living the high life but may be happier than those obsessed with only the standard of life.

Standard of living should not interfere with its quality. If only pursuing outward material things, at the expense of other important things like health, family, spirituality, etc., is what you are all about, then soon you will be forced to slow down when everything comes crashing down.

The best way of living life is to let the quality of life determine the standard, not the other way round. If you will live in a big house, make sure that your finances allow that, and that your health is not jeopardized to get that, and that your family is not sacrificed in the pursuit of that. Pursue quality of life and the standard will take care of itself.

3. Hierarchy:

The way the world operates, and the values that the media, TV, and other worldly sources are offering, gives most people an impression that the spheres of life have a hierarchy. We are made to believe that some cows are more important than others. Most people feel important and successful if they were successful in their career and financial spheres, even when they may not be doing so well in health and family spheres and have terrible relationships. From God's perspective, there is no hierarchy for these spheres; they are all important and they are integrated. Because these spheres are all important and integrated, we live in them simultaneously as a result. When one is not doing well, it will affect the other. The same is true if you take deliberate steps to feed these spheres; as one gets healthy, it may start to lift up another sphere. They are one whole, not the sum of the other. Therefore, when one is neglected it will start a process that will eventually affect the other spheres.

The world has taught us to elevate certain spheres, to our own detriment. When you get your values from popular culture, and have no Biblical worldview, chances are that you will have a hierarchy of these spheres. Some will be more important than others. Which means that, to you, feeding the cows (spheres) you deem important will take priority over the others. This is a recipe for disaster. Sooner or later, you will be forced to get a balance because you will start to experience pain in those areas that you have concentrated on, because the ones you have neglected will start to interfere with the ones you are concentrating on. Unfortunately, when the thin cows start eating the fat cows, don't think that the thin ones will change.

"The thin cows ate up the fat ones, but no one would have known it, because they looked just as bad as before".[26].

---

26. Genesis 41:20-21; Good News Bible

4. Prioritizing:

The biggest mistake most people make is to think that a time will come when they should slow down in one area or even completely stop nurturing it while they are concentrating on another. I have heard people say to me, Pastor, I am so busy, I will only be able to participate at church when things at work slow down. What they are saying to me is that, at the moment, their spiritual lives are on hold. This does not mean that one's spiritual life only requires participating in church activities. Nonetheless, when most people start to give an excuse of this nature, chances are other spiritual disciplines are also on hold. Others have neglected their family because perhaps it is too busy at work. This is a recipe for disaster. The moment you neglect any cow to prioritize another you are quoting trouble. All of the seven cows need feeding.

Nonetheless, having said that all spheres are important and that there is no hierarchy, and that all should be given sufficient time, allow me to say that there are times when we need to give more time than usual to a sphere because it is causing havoc in our lives. This should be communicated to those spheres that will be affected by such a decision, so that they should be able to absorb the pain for a while. However, this should not be forever, but for a given time.

So if, for example, you realize that lack of money is causing havoc in your marriage like it did in mine–sit down with your spouse and children (if you have any) and together set a time that the family should sacrifice to feed the financial cow. You may have to call your mother and siblings and friends to alert them that for such-and-such period of time I will be off the grid for a while to do such-and-such. This helps those in your important relationships to understand when they don't get the right amount of time and attention.

My advice is that before you go out and prioritize a cow, please make sure you are feeding the right cow. As we already said many times in this book, don't concentrate on trying to rescue a cow that is being eaten. Many times, where you are getting the pain is not where your problem is. That sphere is signaling to you that there is a sphere in your life that you have neglected. Make sure you identified the right cow to give more time. If you prioritize a wrong cow, you are adding fuel to the fire.

When I look at my life, I see that if I didn't know this, I would have taken a lot of time in marriage counselling. When my marriage was having problems, I could have spent lots of time seeking marital counselling, but my problem wasn't marital. It was financial. My wife had no problem; it was just that there was so much pressure and she could not just cope. To be honest, if it my wife was not the woman that she is, I would probably be a divorcé by now.

When you solve your problem without identifying the right angry cow, you deal with a symptom, leaving the real problem festering. For me I identified the angry cow as being financial, and when I dealt with it and started to feed the financial cow, my marriage went back to normal because it wasn't the problem, it was just a victim of what was going on in my finances. My strategy was to take a deliberate step, with my wife's full permission, to be away from home on extended periods of time doing those things that earned me some money because my financial sphere was in very bad shape.

5. Physical and Spiritual

Reality is made up of the physical and spiritual._ Our lives are made up of two major components, the physical and the spiritual. These two are not in conflict with each other. The physical and spiritual make up what we call reality. The seven cows fall among one of the two components. One is not more important than the other. To be successful, both should be taken seriously.

What causes confusion in some people's lives is that they either look at the physical to be inferior to the spiritual, or the other way round. They tend to pity one against the other. Our spiritual side of life and that of our physical are both important. Yes I know that some of our physical reality is contaminated by the fall of Adam, still we need to respect the fact that our reality is made up of spiritual and physical, we just have to know how to navigate around the fallen aspects of our physical lives.

Of the seven, health, finances, and career fall within the physical and our relationships, hobbies, family and spirituality fall within the spiritual. We can also call the spiritual intangible. This is the part of our reality that may not be physically seen, but we can experience it. Like a great friendship. While we may not explain why we connect with other people and not with others is immaterial. The truth is that we just click with other people and form lasting friendships.

Our relationships, our hobbies, and our spiritual lives fall in the realm of intangibles. These are spiritual realities. Enjoying someone's company is a spiritual thing, and so is enjoying a hobby. Love, joy, resilience, and all the other intangible virtues fall within the spiritual. We can't physically see them or touch them but these are real things.

Due to lack of understanding of this fact, some people elevate their physical side more and look down on any spiritual reality. Actually some people say that whatever can't be measured is not real. Mostly this is said by people who believe in science. I believe in science, but I also believe that reality is more than just what I can see and measure. They may not take their spirituality as an important aspect of their existence. Many times they do that at their peril. That is why sometimes people that are so into the physical border between lunatic and eccentric. They are usually cold and have personalities that are unapproachable.

There are those whose scales tip on the spiritual side of things who look at anything physical as a necessary evil. They look down on anyone who has a healthy appetite to earn money and improve on their physical lives. They look down on rich people and those that pursue material success in this life. They think such people are worldly. Again this extreme is not healthy. God created both the physical and the spiritual.

Both these approaches to life are wrong. Life is both physical and spiritual and the two make up reality.

If you don't want your cows to eat each other, you need to look at both the physical and the spiritual as important and that these two are not separate from each other but that they make one whole. Look at the cows that fall within the physical to be as important as those belonging to the physical.

6. Scheduling:

We live at a time in human history when busyness is worshipped. Busy people are heroes. Busy people are looked at as successful. While I am all for productivity, I am not one who supports busyness for busyness' sake. Because of the culture of busyness, our schedules are full of those things that the culture deems important and we forget that our schedules should contain activities that feed all the seven spheres. If you look into the schedule of an average person, you will see meetings and activities that have to do with work, but no such activities as going out with friends, or time with the kids, or just time at home doing nothing. These are activities that should only be done for convenience as they wait for important things.

I read an article in *Christianity Today* where Bill Hybels was talking about the importance of filling our schedules not only with those activities that are work-related, but to include even those that have nothing to do with work. He mentioned in the article that we need to take caution because a schedule is not only a set of activities but who we are becoming. He said, "It is not just about what you are accomplishing; it is also about what you are becoming in the process".

If I were to ask, what is in your schedule? Does it include non-work responsibilities? Do you take the non-work responsibilities as seriously as you do the work ones such that they find their way in your diary? Do you think that time with your kids, exercise, your hobbies are as important and should be given space in your schedule as your business or career related activities? Do you feel that these non-work-related activities are just as important as your work-related ones? Would you feel that you are accomplished if your diary has such entries as time with Dad, time to chill with my sister, at home with family playing Monopoly? Obviously those are not things we put in our diaries.

The next time you sit down to schedule your life, look into all the seven spheres of life and allocate activities and time accordingly. While they may not all require the same amount of time, they should all make it into your schedule, and should be accorded the same importance.

7. The myth of Right Time

The biggest myth about time is one which says, "the right time will come for me to spend more time with family, or with friends". Truth be told, if you don't take deliberate steps to nurture certain spheres of your life, they will never be given the attention they need because we are busy people. I recall some time ago when I realized I had not seen one of my friends for the whole year. When we finally got to meet, we both admitted that if we don't take deliberate steps, we will never meet. One needs to purposely set time aside for each one of the seven cows. If you don't, you will starve other cows and that is quoting trouble.

8. Will Power Vs. Commitment:

To succeed at anything, one needs a plan more than one needs willpower. Using willpower to do something is setting yourself up for failure. Willpower wanes; commitment to a plan is always a better bet. A plan will always trump willpower.

In my personal life I have seen that, the times that I have depended on willpower, I have done something on full steam the first few times. After a few weeks or months of doing it, there is a decline in enthusiasm and eventually a death of what I started. However, even without much willpower, when I commit to doing something on a particular time I seem to have more success.

How to Achieve Your Goals

Create an action plan. A good action plan should include:

1. A sphere (cow): all seven cows should find themselves in your schedule. Don't make a

schedule and say you will do hobbies when you have time, or take your wife out on a date when things slow down at work. What you are saying is that your hobbies and your wife are not that important to your life, if that's the case.

2. Goals: Your goals to maintain balance in all spheres should be in written form. Set specific goals in every sphere of your life. When I ask people to show me their goals, it is very rare that I find relationship goals, let alone hobby goals. Set goals in all the seven areas.

3. Activities: Put together actual activities of what you will do on a daily, weekly, or monthly basis to feed a sphere. Goals should be translated into actual activities for them to come to pass. You cannot have elaborate goals that do not translate into activities. Goals should translate into action.

4. Time: Goals and activities are not enough. Every activity should be allocated to the time it should happen. To put it in your schedule or to have it as a goal won't change anything if there is no time attached to it and no specific time allocated.

3.   What was your biggest lesson(s) in this chapter?

....

....

....

....

....

....

....

....

....

....

....

....

4.   How will you apply them to your life?

....

....

....

....

....

....

....

....

....

....

....

....

Success Ratio Quiz

To find out your thin and fat cows, please do an assessment of your life using the 35 questions provided below. Score yourself using a scale of 1 to 5, 1 being the worst and 5 being excellent. Just put your score against the question. At the end of the quiz add up all the scores in each letter. You have questions from A to G. Every area has a total of 25 points, therefore your score will be out of 25.

When you have scored each sphere, add them together and multiply the sum by 100 then divide the added totals by 175 to find your success ratio. The total score in an area will show which areas are fat and which ones are thin.

Add up your score in every letter; this will give you your score in that sphere. Your highest score represents the sphere where you are concentrating and the lowest shows the area that will soon start to eat other sphere. The formula to get the ratio is given below.

Quiz Questions

A. I diligently watch what I eat, and I drink at least six glasses of water per day

B. I regularly read my Bible, and observe a daily routine of personal devotion

C. I have a deliberate plan to deepen my relationship with my family

D. I have a few/a lot of people I can confide in when I have a challenge at a personal level, or with my career/business

E. I know exactly what my hobbies are and I take time to do activities that are related to my hobbies

F. I love my work, and I enjoy doing it.

G. My finances are in order and I know exactly where my money comes from and I keep a record of where it goes

A. I observe a seven-hour or more sleep pattern.

B. I attend a small Bible-based group to nourish my spiritual life

C. I regularly spend time with my family to talk and share life's pleasantries and challenges

D. I have a few/a lot of people I can call true friends

E. I deliberately give time to my hobbies and personal interests

F. I derive joy, happiness and fulfillment from my work

G. I have little or no debt

A. I religiously exercise as a member of a gym, or as a member of a group of friends who exercise together

B. I regularly attend church, and read spiritually uplifting materials to nourish and learn more about my spiritual life

C. I take deliberate steps to connect with my children, my wife/husband, my father, my siblings

D. I love the times I spend with my friends and make an effort to maintain my relationships with them

E. I have a budget specifically for my hobbies and personal interests

F. I love the time I spend at work

G. I save a minimum of 10 % of all the money I earn

A. I watch my stress levels diligently

B. I pray regularly, alone, and sometimes with friends

C. I love family times and enjoy spending time with my family

D. I get a lot of fulfillment from spending time with my friends

E. I take my hobbies seriously as part of my life

F. I enjoy spending time outside work with my work colleagues

G. I am happy with what I am earning, although I would still love to earn more

A. I regularly check my blood pressure, cholesterol, sugar levels, heart and do other important health checks from time to time

B. I often fast and pray to seek God's face and when I am faced with difficult situations to get some answers

C. I have a great relationship with my children, my spouse, my parents, and my siblings

D. I regularly visit friends and they visit me

E. My hobbies are important to me even when they are not to others

F. I know I am doing what I am gifted/talented for

G. Money is important to me and I look at earning money as a normal part life

1. Health =

2. Spirituality =

3. Family =

4. Relationships =

5. Hobbies =

6. Career =

7. Financial =

Total: -----------------------

Success Ratio Formula

Total Score multiplied by 100 and divided by 175 is equal to your success ratio

---

Example

Total Score 120

120 x 100 = 12000

12000 / 175 = 68%

You are 68% successful.

About the Author

Well-respected pastor, consultant, and sought-after speaker Kenneth Mwale has lived a storied life. Born in Zambia, he developed a passion for public speaking and inspiring people and organizations. That drive to enhance the lives of others would be the impetus for what he now recognizes is his calling.

From facilitating workshops, to organizing turnaround processes for government-funded nonprofit organizations, to developing a renowned leadership program, he has made good on his promise to be a beacon of hope for individuals and businesses alike. Believing that balance is the key to success, he has taken his mission a step further by now offering workshops that teach the art of producing profit with spiritual and emotional intelligence.

Kenneth has now parlayed his passion into what he hopes will be a life-changing series of books to help inspire readers worldwide. His first two books, ***Money is not the Problem; People Are*** and ***God is not Religious,*** are available on Amazon.com. ***Balanced on Purpose*** is the next offering in the series.

When not tending to his pastoral duties or holding Life Integration workshops, Kenneth can be found enjoying time with his wife and two young children in Pretoria, South Africa, which has been his new home for the past 16 years.

www.ingramcontent.com/pod-product-compliance
Lightning Source LLC
Chambersburg PA
CBHW061536050726
47593CB00002B/805